roll with it

roll with it

living, working, and parenting
by the seat of your pants

kim z. garrett

BROWN BOOKS
PUBLISHING GROUP

Roll with It

Living, Working, and Parenting by the Seat of Your Pants

Brown Books Publishing Group
16250 Knoll Trail Drive, Suite 205
Dallas, Texas 75248
www.BrownBooks.com
(972) 381-0009

A New Era in Publishing™

ISBN 978-1-61254-177-8
LCCN 2014943337

Printed in the United States
10 9 8 7 6 5 4 3 2 1

For more information or to contact the author, please go to
www.TheElectraZaneProject.com

To my husband.

After all these years, I still have the biggest crush on you. Thank you for believing in me, picking up the pieces of my scattered brain, and putting me on a solid pedestal. You're always going to be the best thing that ever happened to me.

To my boys, Carson and Jack.

No words can describe how proud I am of you every day and how much I love you. I can't wait to watch the men you become—even when you're both old and grey, I'll still call you my babies.

To my Memaw.

You will forever be the most amazing woman I know. Thank you for sharing your wisdom. I love you more than you will ever know! Wouldn't want to change a thing.

contents

acknowledgments

To the heroes in this book—the parents of my friends, teachers, counselors, bosses, clients—thank you. Sometimes we don't realize the impact of one small word of encouragement. All we really need is for someone to believe in us.

The stories shared in this book are from my childhood. I'm happy to say that at sixty, my Memaw woke up, quit smoking cigarettes, and went to school to get her real estate license. She's still hilariously rough and tumble, but she's a reminder that you can turn it around at any age. It's important that I share that even though I am estranged from my mother, I have no anger towards her. I do not judge, and although I will never forget the hurtful things she has done and said to me, I forgave her a long time ago.

To Milli Brown and the outstanding group of professionals at Brown Books Publishing Group—thank you.

introduction

I've worked since I was fifteen years old. It was my escape. By age forty, I had a change of focus—this time from full-time professional to full-time stay-at-home mom, a dream job that gave me the opportunity to be exactly the kind of parent I always wanted to be: the kind with plenty of time to do anything and everything for her kids. But I was immediately shaken with the realization that maybe I was a better mom when I was working. I didn't fit into this mom world. Maybe I was better when I let my job define me. I felt lost. Was I looking for my self-esteem to be fueled by my kids? My husband? I knew any of the above was an unhealthy expectation, but I couldn't shake the feeling that something external had to take on some of the responsibility of defining who I was. And then, I had to figure out how to help my own kids figure out who they were. But how? I organically had something they never will have: adversity. My childhood was filled with it. Don't get me wrong, I like that my life unfolded exactly the way it did, but my reality brings me to my ultimate question: If I'm able to give my kids whatever they want, isn't it my responsibility to also give them obstacles and independence now? While they're young?

So here I am in this book, asking questions and defining answers as best I can:

- Is it our individual upbringing that determines the type of parents we will be?

- Is it the parents that surrounded us that we looked up to and maybe thought, "Now that's the woman I want to be when I grow up"?

- Is it just how we're wired? There are families with six kids—all with the same parents—and yet they each grow up to be very different adults.

- Maybe the partner we chose to grow old with has more to do with it than we think?

- Do we overthink everything? Aren't kids just humans who are genetically wired, and all we really need to do is love them, give them a safe haven and structure, and build character? Time with our kids as kids flies by—do I really want to spend a second of it arguing over seventh-grade math?

I'll admit, it was easier for me to go to work when they were younger because when I was home, I was really home, mentally and physically. I was on the floor building a train set or assembling a 1,200-piece LEGO® Death Star. Now that I'm home all the time, I still do those things, but they seem to have lost some of their importance and significance because they're not separated with a work trip. For example, if you drink champagne every day, does it lose its appeal or reference to some special moment or occasion?

I wonder.

I'm always fascinated with the guilt that comes with parenting. If we're home, we feel like we should be working—setting an example, making money! If we're doing those things, then we're constantly pulled in the direction of "I should be home with the kids—not here. I'm so selfish!"

So, for myself, I've settled somewhere in the middle. I realize that my kids are fine no matter how much or how little I work. They like to see me doing what I deem as "selfish things" because then, to them, I'm human.

The mom I am today is also because of my husband. I'm reminded that the most important part of all of this is that he has always put me unconditionally first. It hasn't always been easy, and I haven't always been the perfect wife. But now that I look back, I realize that without the hard times the good times are just not nearly as good. So I decided to write a book. I wanted to explore for myself and my family as well as anyone who picked up these pages what happens when you forgive, smile, love deeply, work your ass off, and celebrate every day. The results are hard to summarize because they're bigger than words and they grow constantly. But maybe that's what being a parent is all about—taking it all in, embracing your crazy past and exciting future, and accepting the fact your kids are perfectly, wonderfully fine no matter what you do.

I believe we're all better parents when we work from a foundation (even though we don't always have the perfect answer) and accept the fact that sometimes the very best choice is to smile, chill out, and roll with it.

1

a girl walks into a bar

*You can't necessarily control how things
start out, but you sure can make choices
about how they move along.*

See that young girl in the corner of the bar near the row of liquor bottles and spotted beer mugs? Sitting on a well-worn bar stool, wearing bright-red overalls, her messy, long, blonde hair tucked behind her ears as she concentrates on coloring? That girl is me at age six. I have no idea what beer or wine or margaritas taste like. The smell of cigarette smoke mingling with overpowering five-and-dime perfume is normal. I don't wait on customers or listen to them tell their drunken stories about stuff with grown-up words that I'm not allowed to say—I just know that after school I come to Joan's Beer Pump because my grandma owns it and she works here. I drink Shirley Temples all night as I wait for her to clean glasses, slip dollar tips into her bra, and then close up shop so we can go home. Most of the time I just sleep in the beer closet because my grandma is insistent that I get plenty of rest. It's a school night, and tomorrow includes recess and a class birthday celebration with lots of chocolate cake.

My original name was Electra Zane; my hippie parents thought it was "normal," their definition of the word a fuzzy, messy reality. Thanks to my grandma, Electra was squashed from the get-go, and my parents landed on Kimberly. My dad's family still calls me Zane; my mother's family calls me Kimberly. Secretly I think Electra fits the best.

I was tossed into my parents' lives in May 1971 like a teddy bear in a rainstorm. My mom and dad were young, and as many other young adults of the late sixties and seventies, they found their addictions in other smaller packages. I was born straight into that well-known fallacy that people can stay together for the sake of a baby. In other words, my mother genuinely thought she could trap my dad into staying with her, but it didn't work. He left, and my mom was resentful. She never wanted the responsibility of a child, which was made more than clear by the amount of time I was left to fend for myself (always), the amount of care she gave me (none), and the fact that my grandmother (a die-hard, potty-mouthed Jehovah's Witness and practicing bartender) was Super Mom by comparison.

When I was a toddler, I went to live with my grandma permanently. I called her "Memaw." She was my world. Over the years, she taught me to play darts, let me shoot pool with the guys at the bar, and gave me a T-shirt that said "Joan's Beer Pump," which I wore to school at least once a week. I was proud of that shirt because I was proud of my memaw.

I was a skinny, precocious, blue-eyed thing with a big smile and a sense that I wasn't living the dream, but youth didn't allow me to articulate what exactly was off-kilter.

But now I can tell you.

By age seven, I entertained the wayward drunks at the bar with Dolly Parton tunes like "Coat of Many Colors," dancing on the bar and looking out into a crowd of blubbering fiftysomethings who made me feel like I was a superstar. By age eight, I got stoned from eating marijuana brownies. Who knew the large, yummy-smelling pan of chocolate also had a bag of weed in it? By age nine, I wasn't just a latchkey kid—I was a "latchlife" kid.

No one was at my home six out of seven nights a week, so I did what I wanted, and none were the wiser. No one asked to see a report card, no one wondered what I had for dinner, and no one was concerned that I'd be afraid of the dark. I wore my purple corduroy pants with fringe down the sides and a matching purple cowboy shirt all the time, even if they hadn't been laundered. I listened to my *Grease* album over and over. My reality was what I made it, and with no curfew, no rules, and no role models—unbelievably, I made mostly right choices.

By the time I was ten, my grandma and her new husband Huff moved us into a bigger and better house in Fort Worth. The mortgage was paid by the money she made from the Red Barn, a bar she took owner-ship of in 1980.

When Memaw was home, so was her entourage. Ours was the party house. We had pot plants that grew along the back fence, and my grandma and her friends smoked all of the time. As other little girls my age were entertained with their Easy Bake Ovens, I was entertained by Memaw's easily baked pals. I saw so many things in the backyard! But I was happy. I had friends, I had love, and I had the perfect sleepover house because no one was home most nights—and we had cable!

People who come into my life now would never guess how the first half started out. When my mom did decide to resurface—at select school moments where she could aggressively insert herself to demonstrate her motherly authority—it always, without fail, ended in horrible violence. She beat me. She insulted me. She tried to infect me with her poisonous perspective as deeply as possible. She named me as the reason she never made anything of her life, but I knew better. No one makes you do anything. You rise and fall in line with your own beat.

I went on to college, not a resume-making school—Tyler Junior College—but at least I got admitted. I'd never been a good student, so a green light to junior college was a victory. But even there, in an academic setting, I just didn't care about grades or homework or learning anything that didn't interest me in the moment. I made a ton of friends at that school—some I still have to this day. I left school before the end of the second year with my first broken heart, determined not to let some guy make me feel bad about myself. I transferred to the University of North Texas in Denton, not sure what I was going to wind up doing professionally. That summer, a friend suggested I apply for a job leasing apartments, and within a few months, they asked if I could move to Dallas. I hit the big time! I loved Dallas. I had friends, lots of new people to chat with, and I was good at my job. I met my best friend Danny there, and he would also become my husband, even if he didn't know it at the time. He sauntered in to lease an apartment, and I coyly explained that the only available unit was the one that just happened to be next to mine. The rest, as they say, is romantic history.

The same year my other neighbor invited me to a party, and, by happenstance, I met the general manager of Texas Stadium and the Dallas Cowboys. He was a sweet man, and he offered me a job as his administrative assistant. I didn't care what the title was, and I definitely did not care what it paid. In one short year, my life took a 180-degree turn. I was in charge of the suites at the stadium. For every sponsor I met, I smiled and made friends. One of the sponsors in specific was Riddell—the company that makes football helmets. They actually had an athletic footwear division, and within a year, they offered me a job as their director of marketing. Yep, me—the one who barely graduated high school, the one without a college degree, and the girl who received the "Biggest Airhead" award at my high school. Director of marketing! Most of my friends were still in college.

I made my way from Riddell to Clear Channel Communications where I sold ads for local radio stations to selling sponsorships at House of Blues, a popular concert-and-entertainment venue. From there, I went back to Clear Channel, lured by the title of vice president and a bigger paycheck. Then in 2007, I received a call from a recruiter with Facebook, a company I'd never heard of before. I flew out to Palo Alto for the interview. It went well, but I couldn't wrap my head around an advertising platform. How could they monetize this idea of a social community, this memory book of sorts? At the airport headed back to Dallas, I stopped at a gift shop. Among the rows of magazines was *Fast Company,* and there on the cover was Mark Zuckerberg. By the time I landed, I knew I had to get that job. Thirteen interviews later, I did. I opened Facebook's central sales region that year— working from home. Facebook, I believed, was poised to be enormous.

I worked as Director of National Sales for Facebook for more than four years, nose to the grindstone, racking up stock options. When I was fully vested with the company in 2011, I took a long, deep look at my financial options, talked with my advisor and husband, and came to the conclusion that now was an ideal time to make a move. I cashed in my hearty collection of stock and pinched myself. At age forty, I could officially retire and never again have to work for income.

adversity, anyone?

I believe that adversity does one of two things to a person: it beats you down, or it lifts you up to a greater level you would never have thought possible. My adversity did the latter. A friend of mine from child-hood recently contacted me and told me she was in therapy to help her deal with unfortunate events from her childhood. She explained that those incidents are what messed her up as an adult. A mutual male friend of both of our moms had taken naked pictures of the two of us as very young girls—I do remember that, but my memory stops there. She suggested I try therapy as well to help me reconcile my relationship with my mother and my previous lifestyle—a lifestyle that included a childhood with days where I had to eat dog food with ketchup or go hungry.

But I think the brain forgets things to protect the spirit. I have zero desire to dredge up anything that isn't an easily fetched memory. I'm happy with what I remember. I've learned from what I didn't forget. I also do not blame my mother, my father, or my grand-mother—life is funny, and I wouldn't change a thing. I am who I am because of them, and I refuse to judge them from where I am today. You just never know.

To this day, I still have my Joan's Beer Pump T-shirt. I still remember eating tuna out of the can. And even now, the smell of pot at a concert makes me laugh because I can still see Memaw in the backyard holding a watering can, making sure her "sanity" was nurtured.

We all have our own stories to tell. Some seem, on the surface, more interesting than others. I'm sure there are few, if any, little girls who could expertly chalk a pool cue while watching *Fat Albert* cartoons. Now I'm a woman of success. I embrace every day that I've been given, and I don't say that lightly. For all intents and purposes, I've made it. Now I must stop and ask myself, "How will that translate for my children?"

And there you have it: the question that sparked the idea for this book. If I could take everything that happened to me—the good and the not-so-good—and find a way to demonstrate the wisdom or questions or observations that came from all of it, not only would my own children have a record of why mom and dad do certain things, believe certain things, and stress certain things, but I could also start a conversation with other parents.

If you want parenting advice, you need only a computer and a search engine. There's tons of advice out there. I'm here to discuss what I've seen work and not work. I'm here to share my questions and concerns. And I'm here because I'm a mom who doesn't have the answers for everyone—but I do have insights.

My husband and I can give our children anything. Everything. How should we balance this world of privilege with lessons in grace and humility? As I observe the lives of my two boys, I often see the gaps from my own upbringing. I do my best to fill in the holes so their lives are packed sky high. They are in the privileged position of having parents with deep financial resources, of not ever having to go hungry, and of never worrying about sleeping in a beer closet. But these facts don't necessarily mean they'll turn out better or worse than I did. They just mean that this is their truth, their road. My role is to move them along, to give them guidance, to make them stop and think. But my job is also to get out of their way.

I've taken a step back to observe our parenting style and beliefs. I've watched others. And while I certainly don't think I have all of the parenting answers, I do think it's important to share thoughts and strategies with those willing to listen. We live in a different world than when I was a little girl. My story is dramatically different from most. And while my personal situation now comes with abundant resources, we all live in a nation where opportunities abound. So I wonder every day, *How can we raise our kids with privilege—without ruining them?*

Being successful sometimes means getting invited to important parties. Often they're the fancy kind. So I wear my Christian Louboutin heels and feel elegant in my Gucci cocktail dress. My husband tells me I look stunning. I believe the most important choice in life is who one marries, and I know with absolution that I hit the jackpot. And as I walk the room, holding Danny's arm, smiling at the other guests and sharing pleasantries, I'm keenly aware of all of the story lines, vantage points, and incidents that got me to this very moment.

And no matter who's at the party, no matter how gorgeous the décor, or no matter how exquisite the food, I still feel much more real somewhere else—outside the doors of the fancy party, my shoes kicked off, my hair pulled back into a ponytail, and laughing like crazy as I crack jokes with the valet.

2

my heroes have always been cowboys

*To be a hero, one doesn't have to
hold a basketball or a high note.*

When I was young, single-digit young, the definition of hero was lost on me. Good people were the ones who helped others. I identified these good people by the reactions to their presence. For instance, when I saw my memaw pull out $5 from her wallet and hand it to a homeless guy lounging on the sidewalk near her bar, I could tell by his shocked smile that she did something good. I saw that he recognized her as kind. I wanted people to have that same reaction to me.

I looked up to people I was around daily, people like a girl in my class who had the sweetest manners toward everyone. My friend's parents who smiled and hugged me when I visited and gave me hot chocolate with loads of marshmallows at slumber parties. My teachers who led the book drives; the one who told me I could come to her office to talk any time.

I made no connection between hero and fame or money or some special talent. Everyone at my memaw's bar—the Red Barn—had a blue-collar job. No one was rich, no one had social status, and no one knew anything about expensive ties or five-star dining. The people at the bar were nice to me and to each other in a real way. These were the beer-drinking guys with oil under their nails and dusty work pants that would see a washing machine only on Fridays. They came to the bar to relax, to talk to Memaw, and to feel a sense of place. She knew everyone by name.

In the bar, I overheard conversations about "feeling lost" or "looking for a better gig" or references to "in prison," but no matter what these guys talked about, Memaw leaned in and listened, nodding to show she understood. Some of the guys at the bar were war veterans and told stories about their time in the service. Memaw asked questions about their experiences, their injuries, and if they killed anyone. She knew something about every person in the bar, and that's why everyone loved her. I learned a lot about people from watching her.

My takeaway: a hero or role model is defined by showing simple kindness.

The Red Barn was also a hangout for motorcycle gangs—leather-wearing, black-T-shirted dudes with red bandanas, chain wallets, and ass-kicking riding boots. If anyone needed a place to stay, and some often did, Memaw invited them to our house. These motorcycle riders were just a bunch of men and women who loved the freedom of wind-slapped hair and the roar of a motor. I have no idea where the connection between danger and motorcycle riders came from; these people were friends. They cleaned their dishes, put their beer bottles in the trash can, and along with everyone else, laughed all the time. They were the salt of the earth; they just enjoyed their days. And they were always, unequivocally, nice to me.

My takeaway: a hero or role model is defined by one's ability to enjoy simplicity.

My heroes have also always been the people who built our country—those men and women who work in construction to build houses and malls, assemble automobiles, and work as plumbers, electricians, postal workers—people who aren't afraid to climb a telephone pole or prune the enormous trees lining the roads and the ones who build our roads and repair our roofs. I think it takes a certain amount of discipline to have a skilled-labor career. And my hat is off to the required sweat equity and physical demands these professionals can handle. Sometimes I think we send the wrong message about these jobs—that they aren't desirable because they don't require a four-year degree, pay six figures, or demand an Einstein-like intellect. But these jobs are precise in their beauty—they are focused and specialized and important. Not everyone needs to go to college. Thank goodness for that.

In the news, heroes are people who take action to save a life: running into a burning building, diving into the lake to save someone from drowning, or lifting a crashed car off of an unconscious victim pinned underneath. In our culture, our heroes are people who have amassed great success: Wall Street winners, pro ballers, movie stars, supermodels, socialites, and singing-competition winners. Since when has it become a coveted, idolized skill to be able to sing? How many singing shows does one prime time need? It seems like every single one them can sing, so how about a reality show to cure cancer or build a solar-powered rocket? I'm not a fuddy-duddy. I love music, art, and reality television, but our kids confuse the concept of fame with the idea of what a role model should be. Quiz grade-schoolers on what they want to be when they grow up:

A. Engineer

B. Pop star

C. Surgeon

D. Teacher

And then call me if there's not a circle around B.

As a parent, I struggle with the notion that fame is heroic. I want my children—and all children—to strive and work and reach high, but I want that idea to be grounded. You can be anything you want to be. ~~True.~~ Trueish.

The child who can't hold a note isn't going to be a singing sensation. Rather than looking at what we can do to propel our kids into the spotlight, to help them realize dreams of fame and fortune, magazine covers, and Internet domination, why don't we strive toward helping them achieve a state of mind?

"So, sweetheart," says the mother to her son, "what do you want to be when you grow up?"

The son stops racing his toy car across the carpet and looks up. "Happy," he responds. Then he's off again with his car.

That's my idea of bliss.

I'm not hopping on the anticelebrity bandwagon or stopgapping anyone's desire to be a star or a jet setter. I wonder if it might be a more productive approach for us parents, friends, family, and adults to ask questions of our kids to find out why they want this road. Is it for the attention? Is it narcissism? We all want the first, and we already have the latter. After all, attention and narcissism are two of the reasons Facebook is so popular. We want to post and share things that are important or funny or interesting or revealing because humans need to disclose. The attention and feedback we receive is exciting and fun and makes us feel proud and heard and recognized. That's narcissism. And in small doses this formula is perfect. Give it out in big doses, and we've created a monster in diva's clothing.

My takeaway: a hero or role model is defined by one's ability to strive for happiness.

mrs. miller and more

Mrs. Miller was a high school counselor who lived on my street. In the middle of my sophomore year, she called me into her office. "Let's talk about those motorcycles in front of your house," she said with a suspicious look. "On Tuesday, there were thirty-five of them parked on the street. Lots of loud noise coming from inside. What's going on at home, Kim?"

So I told Mrs. Miller the truth with a shrug, "Memaw's friends stopped by, and we had a party."

Mrs. Miller asked more questions. I answered honestly. I wasn't sure what the big deal was, unless she was concerned I wasn't getting to bed early enough with all the people and music.

As I painted the picture of our party house, Mrs. Miller stopped me midsentence. "Look at me in the eyes, Kimberly. You're coming across as dingy because you keep glancing at the door and around the room.

You're looking everywhere but at me. People will think you're lying if you don't look at them when you're talking."

"But I'm not lying," I replied.

"I know you're not. But others might think you are."

Mrs. Miller recognized that I was uncomfortable with looking people in the eyes, so she called me out on it to help me. "Also, you need to sit up. Your posture is a sign of confidence."

Immediately I straightened up. I liked feeling taller. And I liked Mrs. Miller for showing me the importance of being forthright.

As I grew up, several other "Mrs. Millers" were there for me—people who gave me unsolicited advice, pulled me along, or encouraged me. I must've seemed pitiful to so many: the little girl with the messed up, drug-dependent mother; the child who spent more time in a bar playing with swizzle sticks than with baby dolls; the sweet, young thing who wore the same clothes week after week and never watched *Sesame Street* or *Charles in Charge*. But I wasn't pitiful. You only know what you know, so my own disconnection with what was then a "normal childhood" didn't hit home until I had a glimpse much later of what my life should've included.

An example of my discovery of "normal" started in kindergarten. Beginning that year, the family across the street had me over for dinner several times a week. Through these invitations, I learned what dinnertime conversation meant. My Blue Bird counselor regularly picked me up from school, so I didn't have to walk home. My dance instructor gave me a ride to recitals. And when I was in the Miss Junior Fort Worth pageant, my dance instructors and the other girls' moms cheered me on from backstage because no one from my own family was there.

My friends' parents gave me guidance. One mom showed me how to apply eye cream. Another taught me how to cook macaroni. And another one offered point-blank wisdom that I understood only as a woman: "Never be a slut, Kim. Anyone can be a slut. It takes a real lady to say no, and those are the type of girls who find good men." I giggled when she said slut. It sounded funny coming from a grown-up.

In high school, I learned social norms from my friends and was treated to what I call that "little mom stuff" from their parents. For example, my boyfriend's mom took us to the movies and showed me what should be considered a delicacy—mixing popcorn with chocolate almonds. She taught me how to decorate a Christmas tree, beginning with ornaments, then lights, and then the star. I'd never had a Christmas tree, so for all I knew, they grew in the forest with popcorn garlands. Much of the mom stuff I learned from others, I do with my own kids today.

I'm positive that the wings I nuzzled under happened because these women saw things in me—things that alerted them—and they knew they needed to step in with advice. I'm so glad they did. Their voices had a profound effect. At high school graduation, Memaw and Huff clapped and whistled. But I could hear the other moms cheering too.

My takeaway: A hero or role model is someone who intuitively steps in because she recognizes discord.

going way out there

I was the kind of fired-up little girl, teenager, adult, and now forty-something who always tried new things and did new things without a push or encouragement from anyone in my own family. I was loved, yes, but not parented.

Throughout my life, the people clapping and cheering were my teachers or other parents, all who went out of their way—way out of their way—to help me with logistics, costumes, encouragement—all of it. My memaw gave me her bar profits to pay for dance lessons or gymnastics classes, but the buck stopped there. To everyone who did the heavy lifting for me, I hope I said thank you. I'm not sure that I did. As I said, you only know what you know, and the village raising me was my "normal," so I didn't recognize their efforts at the time as over and above.

Even my friends stepped in when I was in need of parenting. For example, in high school I better understood my mother's destructive effect, but she still had her pull on me. You're always that little girl, that little boy, that child who's under a parental spell. With every phone call and stress-laced interaction, I had this hint of hope that she'd magically turn into the mother I wanted. I weathered the disappointment like a pro. It became a habit.

On any given evening, after a shouting match with my mother that always escalated into physical contact, I'd call Bart, one of my best friends. I would open the window in my bedroom, sneak out, and wait on the curb for him to pick me up. He'd drive, and I'd yell and cry. Oh, how I cried. Bart never told a soul about our evening sessions. He was just my friend.

My takeaway: A hero or role model is defined by the ability to simply listen to someone in need.

As a teenager, once I started working, I didn't stop. My first job was in a karate studio gift shop and then a country club day care. I waited tables at several restaurants which, by the way, is the very best experience you can get—you learn how mean people can be and how amazingly generous at the same time—a metaphor for real life. I leased apartments, worked retail, including at sports stores, shoe stores, and fashion shops. I could go on. I never asked questions, I never whined, and no job was beneath me. Like most of my generation, I was so happy to be working because I knew that, in order to get where I wanted to be, I needed stepping-stones, experience, contacts, and practice. All along the way, my bosses took notice. My clients became friends. I applied the lessons I learned watching my grandmother at the Red Barn. Many of the people in my professional past are still my friends today.

As a mother, I push and guide my kids toward the types of heroes I want them to learn from. Mothers and fathers have a strong influence—the largest, most long-lasting influence, if the role is applied. Aunts, uncles, family, friends, and even casual acquaintances can make a difference too. You never know how your sound bite, shared philosophy, or quick word of wisdom will linger. To that end, I'm keenly aware of my own ability to influence someone else, not to control someone else but to provide a hand. So I keep my eyes open, watching and listening for today's version of me—the person who needs a word of encouragement—who's open to a quick bit of unsolicited, worldwide guidance—the one who craves that subtly important nudge toward positive action.

3

what doesn't help you makes you stronger

Self-worth isn't defined by the things you accomplish—it's how you feel about yourself as you accomplish things.

The distinction between self-worth and self-importance took a good while to define. For a long time, I confused the two. Now I define self-worth as that sense of value one has for oneself. I think self-worth comes from the pride of accomplishment, whether it's learning a new recipe, finishing a load of laundry after a crazy busy day, landing a new job, teaching your child the piano, or even learning to fly an airplane.

I think self-importance is realizing that you matter—not more than anyone else—as much as everyone else. When I stand back and look at daily life through the lens of establishing self-worth and illustrating that I know I'm important, I'm overwhelmed at the examples. To keep things straight:

Self-worth is seeing/feeling/knowing your personal value.

Self-importance is seeing that others recognize your value.

Both help to define your personal brand, which helps you carve out your way in the world and also helps to establish a pattern for how you'll influence your children to do the same.

I don't pretend to have everything figured out. Our interpretations about ourselves, others, and the collective society change with new experiences and age. But the reason I'm going on about this is that I've learned that both self-worth and self-importance, in balance, are vital to our survival.

So, as the sentiment goes, if I can share these thoughts and help just one person—either by association or because they wildly disagree with me—then my job here is done.

step first, leap later

I did not, by any sense of any definition, have a charmed childhood. My mother was absent for most of my life, or when she was present, she announced "I've arrived!" by beating the hell out of me. Should I have felt bad about myself for her behavior? Was I black-eyed and bruised because I was unworthy and bad? I let her hit me, yell at me, and kick me when I was down. And then, when she was finished—had it all out of her system—I picked myself up and went where I felt loved and appreciated. Maybe it was at Memaw's bar. Maybe at a friend's house. Maybe I visited the school counselor. I recognized the need to be around positive influences. So that's exactly what I did.

As I grew up, I watched as my grandmother enabled my mother. No one took her aside to slap sense into her. Rather, my mother continued doing drugs, she continued living off of government assistance, and she continued blaming everyone else for her mistakes and lot in life. So this got me thinking: What is the point in being here if someone else is constantly taking care of you? What's your personal purpose?

I think it's easy to understand that self-worth is shaped by the way you feel when you accomplish things, when you pay your dues, work hard, and succeed. Often success is a tiered phenomenon, reliant upon stepping-stones. For example, when I worked in radio, I was the assistant to the general sales manager. One day, one of his highest-paid, hotshot sellers strolled past my desk, catching my attention. "Mr. Brown," I said from behind my computer, "you're wearing one black shoe and one brown one."

He looked down. "You're right." We had a laugh. "Well let's hope no one else notices."

That moment was one of the times that I realized the beauty of working your way up the ladder and how those first jobs and occasions are platforms to bigger and better things. Here was a guy making 100,000 times what I was making, and he was just as human as the rest of us. So maybe he was more educated than I was, drove a much nicer car than I did, and took more exotic vacations than I could. I wasn't the one wearing mismatched shoes.

I believe that self-worth, the value you give yourself, is also defined by your failures. If my grandmother had left my mother's failures alone, if she had stopped fueling her habits and behaviors, maybe my mother would've been better for it. But I get why Memaw gave in. As parents, we want to protect our kids from failing. In relationships, we want to protect our husbands and wives and partners from failing. As friends, we want to protect our friends from failing. But what if we, on occasion, step aside?

Self-worth has a chance to develop when you fail, hit rock bottom, think life as-you-know-it is over, but then things change—for the better. It's the little, spotted calf who falls down when he tries to walk. He stumbles, falls, and hits his nose on the dirt, but he picks his head up, drinks his milk, and grows a bit. Little by little, he gets stronger and stronger until he can keep pace with his brothers and sisters in the herd.

Allowing failure—welcoming adversity—is important.

We are all insecure. I look at it like this: every day we have to feed our physical bodies with food so we feel energetic, healthy, and balanced. In that same vein, every day we have to fill our personal bucket. We do things that make us feel good, alive, important, influential, and authoritative. When we go too far, when we try too hard to be self-important, when we don't strike a balance, out comes conceit, misbehavior, insecurity, or underachievement.

How many times have you noticed on Facebook that someone changed his or her profile picture, and that it was obvious that the reason was to look good? I'm as guilty as anyone else of sharing selfies. If I think I look cute or am doing something fun or funny, I am prone to post the image on Facebook or text it around my circle. I want a positive reaction. This is an innocent way to foster self-importance. I want to hear what others think. I want their reactions because they make me feel good. I'm looking for validation that I'm important. No harm, no foul—in small doses. But we can all go overboard.

I've also seen people who rely on self-importance to help define their self-worth. For example, do you remember that girlfriend in high school who was happy only when she had a boyfriend? She'd drop everything and everyone if he called. She'd blow off plans if he wanted to hang out. She felt like she was valuable only when he was giving her attention. That's an imbalance between self-worth and self-importance. I think we need to have validation and inclusion from others in our lives. We need to be able to fit in where appropriate and to be a part of something bigger than ourselves, but at the end of the day, our real character is defined by our self-worth.

I hope I'm not muddying the psychological waters when I say the exact opposite here: I also think there's an appropriate time when you MUST push yourself forward in the minds of others to make them recognize your importance. Please let me explain.

when a bully pushes, push back

In my childhood, just like the childhoods before it, there were bullies. Some of today's most successful artists, musicians, CEOs, and parents were bullied. I was bullied. My best friend, Toni, and I were followed home from school all the time by school bullies. There were times when they threw rocks at our heads. They called my friend "four eyes," and I was bullied by association. I was her friend, and if they were going to throw rocks at her, then I was standing by to take the hit too. They were mean and acted like losers, but at that specific time, they were the cool kids, and they ruled by fear.

I don't think the fact that someone bigger and louder and meaner than me pushed me around when I was a kid can be pinpointed as the reason I've succeeded. It was a period in life, a point of passage. It may have, at the time, pushed me to walk home a new way or prompted me to play on the swings instead of the monkey bars, but that's where I met the girl who would become one of my best friends. My point is that bullying, while not at all fun at the time, can be fuel for greatness. It has a butterfly effect. It's a pushing-off point. It's a testing moment. It's the specific action that will yield a life lesson. Being bullied can help define who we are and help us establish to others that we matter. We are all bigger than the bullies. And I think that's the whole point.

As a parent, I wish I didn't have to accept that bullies are out there, to anticipate that they are going to rear their ugly heads in my boys' lives. While bullies succeed because they prey on the weak, as parents, we can't always level the playing field for our kids. When I was growing up, kids used three-way calling to bully. One kid would call another kid while a third silently listened in, and then, as secrets were divulged or ugly words exchanged, the target would feel embarrassed or shamed, but when they hung up the phone, it was over. There was no tangible trace. Today kids are bullied and the embarrassments are immortalized in social media platforms like Instagram, Facebook, and Twitter. It's a different ball game now. And then what happens is that these kids believe they are the product of their digitized lives because it's the way that others define them. Kids can't recognize that what's online is only an edited version of the person. It's a movie without the parts that happen in between. For example, if a teenage girl posts a photo online of herself in a bikini, then she becomes the girl in the bikini. And while that might be great for a fortysomething to be known for (I'd love to volunteer), it's certainly not the best representation for a teenager.

How do we stop bullying? That's the million-dollar question. But if it happens, demonstrating self-importance needs to kick in. In this instance, it helps to fuel self-worth.

survival instinct

You know how people say, "You have to love yourself so others will love you?" After we roll our eyes, mime exaggerated vomiting, and call them dorky, we all concede that what's truly being said is this: you must have a foundation of self-worth in order for others to recognize your importance. I don't know the major formula for uncovering self-worth, other than to start at the point of survival. What do you need to survive? What do your children need to survive? I'm not talking about the physical needs but rather the emotional survival needs. When push comes to shove, we will all fight for our physical survival—we're wired that way. If you and I were stranded on a mountain, and you died, I'd eat you. "Yay!" I'd say. "You died first! Now I'll have dinner!"

But beyond that, how do you survive? What do you need, and what do your children need to feel their purpose and potential?

I have a friend who's one of the most amazing people I know. But I get this feeling that she's not confident with who she is. I want to take her by the shoulders and ask her why—ask her who sent her negative messages that she believed. I can't understand why she doesn't feel better about herself. But it's obvious that she doesn't because she's settling for a job she's overqualified for; one that pays her much less than she deserves because she's scared to dust off her resume and compete for another position. She's gorgeous and smart and has that "it" factor you notice immediately upon talking with her. But she doesn't see it. She behaves in line with how she views her self-worth. And really, it's all beneath her potential.

own it or run from it

Part of what feeds self-worth is recognizing your strengths and owning them. It's also recognizing your weaknesses and either using them to your advantage or doing whatever you can to distance yourself from them.

When I worked at Facebook, I was surrounded by geniuses—twenty-year-olds with PhDs, Harvard degrees, and fluency in several languages. Facebook's chief operating officer, Sheryl Sandberg, the woman who wrote the book *Lean In: Women, Work, and the Will to Lead,* was very involved with the sellers and attended several meetings and events with me.

Every day I worried that someone would figure out I wasn't formally educated and that I wasn't in the same league on an intelligence quotient. I was always afraid of saying the wrong thing, the dumb thing, or otherwise revealing my insecurities. I think Sheryl had me figured out. She asked me for my observations and insights regarding sales. She played to my strengths. So I owned it. I owned knowing what I knew. I owned being the Southern woman with the fun personality and the blonde hair and the big smile who sometimes said dingy things because it worked for me. It was honest, real, and helped define who I was in the business world. I could talk to any c-level executive without feeling intimidated. People could relate to me. I was likeable. Maybe no one realized I'd been up since 2:00 a.m. completing spreadsheets, answering e-mails from Dell and JCPenney chief marketing execs, or participating in global meetings, but it was OK. I was respected. I leveraged the snapshot version that people saw. I was able to exert my importance, be recognized for my importance, and then recognize my worth. They all work together.

Self-worth and self-importance come together to help define a personal brand. It helps people recognize who they are and helps explain their roles. Helping kids establish their personal brand comes from a hands-on approach. We guide them toward accomplishments and through failures. I don't believe every child deserves a blue ribbon. There's a last place for a reason—so they can try harder next time to move up. I don't believe every person should go to college or strive to be CEO or deserve to be on *America's Got Talent.* My responsibility is to show my children that any of these scenarios is OK. They might become world-class surgeons, or they may become low-brow comedians.

Are they happy? Do they value themselves? Do they value others? Do they have a purpose? As long as they own it, I've done my job.

4

home economics

*When your child complains about not
getting a toy, tell him the truth: "Dude,
there's no more room on the floor."*

When I share the fact that my husband and I
can give our kids anything they want, I do
so with the intent of providing a basis for
my belief that no matter how much privilege children
have, adversity can be a key to creating balance. This
is the reason my goal is to offset that privilege with
something completely opposite. If you have financial
wealth, then material-related adversity has to be
manufactured. In other words, sometimes we have to
make an effort not to give our kids everything they
want. We have to create obstacles to make them work
harder. We have to manufacture ways to make them

demonstrate the demand before we give them the supply. It's our own version of home economics.

With things, from toys to travel to adventure, my husband and I make a concerted effort to set guidelines. We want our children to understand that they need to take stock of the entire picture of their lives—they must take timeouts to realize what they have. It's a type of stop-and-smell-the-roses philosophy but with video games and dirt bikes. This checks-and-balances plan for our family provides a foundation from which our sons can grow into the men we want them to become. We want our children to examine what they have, account for it, and understand that they're fortunate. Not everyone has a swimming pool and a nine-hole putting green in their own backyard. Reality for children is grounded in their surroundings. When I was a kid, I had no idea that wearing an adult-sized Joan's Beer Pump T-shirt probably wasn't appropriate attire. I didn't understand that having a backyard full of pot plants was out of the norm. My reality was comprised of whom and what I was around. This is precisely why I don't want my boys to think everyone lives in a house like ours or that every child on the planet is lucky enough to vacation in Carmel or Costa Rica or vacation at all, for that matter. If my children think that every kid has the latest iPad, then I've done them a disservice as a parent. If my children think they "should have" or are entitled to have a TV and a computer in their room, then I've failed to deliver the proper message. And if I never make my kids work for what they want, not necessarily just to understand the value of a dollar but to understand the value of privilege, then I've most certainly failed as a role model.

So how do you teach children with privilege the importance of adversity? No parents want their kids to struggle or go without. But adversity teaches gratitude, a work ethic, and humility. Money comes and goes. Lessons stay put.

Privilege isn't just about having money. There's the inherent privilege of being born healthy with access to great education, freedom, and societal perks. I know children who are spoiled rotten without having grand homes or game rooms stocked with toys. But it's my belief that, regardless of how you personally define what having privilege means to you, children are better equipped as people when they understand that not everyone is as fortunate as they are.

Every family has its own way of doing things, from setting dinnertime to setting the holiday table. But when grounding our kids, we make an effort to keep their feet planted—and their egos in check. Here are seven ways we do it.

no. 1: demonstrate the importance of sweat equity

When Danny's father passed away, he left his son a 200-acre working ranch with seventy-five head of Hereford cattle and horses. For Danny, there is no greater sanctuary. He's forever working on projects, and the boys see the proof of his hard work: his boots are always caked with mud, his hands are calloused, and he always smells like diesel fuel and cow manure when he comes home. However, every Sunday when Danny walks through our door, he's got a smile from ear to ear and a story to tell. "I'm saving our big oak trees one at a time—trimming them and cutting off the mean briars. They look so happy when I leave, and that makes me happy!" Danny loves trees—I call him the tree whisperer.

That ranch, with all its requisite back-breaking labor, is precious to my family. Our boys know that if anything were to happen to their dad, they'd be responsible for keeping the ranch going. They'd have to pull together to burn the brush, bail the hay, mow the fields, feed the cows, and split wood and stack it. They know the work would fall on them. And as much as they claim to dread it, they also take pride in it. Truth be told, if I ever mutter, "That ranch is too much work; we should sell it," all hell breaks loose.

"That is Papa's ranch!" Jack exclaims.

"We'll never sell it!" Carson adds.

"Never, ever, EVER!" is usually how the exchange ends.

I wanted to explain the place this ranch has in our family to provide context for what happens next. One day Carson was in the playroom. He threw a toy called a Beyblade, a round metal toy that should be on the ground—and definitely not in the air, directly at their big-screen TV. The surface cracked like a spider web. When Carson told us what happened, we didn't yell at him, although I wanted to. Instead Danny sat him down.

"You've got two choices," Danny explained. "One, never play Xbox or Wii again or two, you'll work for a replacement TV by going to the ranch with me for four Sundays in a row for eight hours each day—that's thirty-two hours. I'll pay you $12 an hour to split and stack wood. That'll pay for half of your TV. Your mom and I will pay for the other half."

Carson blinked. "I'll take two."

He had no idea what thirty-two hours would actually look and feel like.

After working that first Sunday, he came home, went straight to the shower, and then to bed. He didn't even stop to eat dinner. The mom in me was worried—were we being too hard on him? What if he hurts himself? Those who know firsthand the actual work behind splitting and stacking wood will understand—the job makes for a rough and monotonous day. Not only is the chore physically difficult, the weather was cold and blustery. Carson wore a hat and gloves like his daddy, and he was still cold. But guess what? That boy never complained. He never tried to shortchange his shift. He never questioned why he had to put in the sweat equity. By the fourth Sunday, he knew his reward was coming, and that morning Carson was dressed and ready at 6:00 a.m. to head out.

The day we came home with the replacement TV, Carson was beaming. He shouted, "I bought that!" The pride and confidence boost he got from accomplishment translated into my own pride. Seeing your children recognize their own self-worth is greater than a trillion brand-new TVs.

no. 2: show them enough is enough

For any parent who's been to the toy aisle at Target, you know there's an impressive assortment of LEGO® sets. We go to Target when the boys have saved money or if they've been especially good, and I want to give them a reward. This particular January, we were going because they had both saved their birthday money and although each one only had $40 left—their words, not mine—they wanted a new LEGO toy. Their birthdays bookend Christmas. Within a three-week time span, we have three celebrations, so our home overflows with new gifts this time of year. My husband and I exchange comforting statements to help rationalize that it's OK to give them so many gifts right up against a major holiday. "It is their birthdays," we tell each other. "If they were born in March, they'd get gifts."

But I have to be honest—watching them expect to be showered with presents is unsettling. I have yet to find that ever-elusive compromise with birthday and Christmas gifts. Maybe I will in time, but we're all a product of our past, and the fact that, as a child, I didn't have gift-filled Christmases has greatly influenced my present-buying behavior.

Now to get back to that January afternoon. With their $40 each, they race to the toy area. I will admit that there's a bit of happy anticipation in it for me too because I love that they'll sit together for hours, follow directions, and build something that consists of 1,200 pieces. When they find the sets they want, they ask if they can each have $20 more. They want the larger-sized LEGO box, which costs $49.99, and with the tax, the total will be close to $60.

"No," I tell them. "You should've saved your other money if you really wanted that."

They huddle. Exchange nods. They then grab two smaller LEGO sets and run to the cashier.

I stroll through the store with a smile and a warm feeling of success. The boys pay for their toys, and we load up and head home. And then the bubble bursts.

"I wish we had had more money for the castle and spaceship."

"Yeah, I know. I don't even really want this one."

I resist looking into the rearview mirror because I'm so angry, and I don't want them to see my eyes. After all of the presents they just received from us, from Santa, and from their grandparents, they have the nerve to say something like that? And especially when there are toys that are still in their boxes! I make a quick mental list of presents they received. I relive the conversations Danny and I had as we planned their birthday parties. I remember being so tired the morning after I stayed up really late to wrap their presents so they could have the perfect Christmas that I missed the mug when I poured my coffee.

And they want the bigger LEGO set?

Oh, hell no.

As the complaints swirled, I pulled over to a Goodwill drop-box site. Without a word, I got out of the car, opened the back door, removed the two LEGO sets from the backseat, and walked over to the box. With one hand I pulled down on the handle. As the trapdoor creaked open, I slid the LEGO sets down the chute with the other. I turned, got back into the car, and resumed driving. Neither said a word for a few minutes. Then I hear this:

"Mom, what did you just do?"

"Oh, well, honey, I heard you say you didn't even want that LEGO set, and it breaks my heart to think of all the little boys who didn't even have a Christmas, much less birthdays with toys flowing out of their closets." I keep my eyes on the road. If I make eye contact, I may raise my voice, and I want to keep calm. "I'd rather they have that LEGO set than to force you have to have something you don't even want. Feel good about yourselves, boys—you just spent your birthday money to put a smile on a little boy's face."

My gaze forward, we drove home in silence. They want to build castles, and that's fine. But I'm building character first.

no. 3: stick to your guns

One particular night, Jack got upset because he didn't get to pick what we were having for dinner. First, a disclaimer: I don't usually let my kids dictate what I make for dinner, but there are occasions when I ask them what they'd like, and then I cook accordingly. So that means one gets macaroni and cheese, another gets a hamburger, and I'll make a salad for me. I'm sure most parents reading this book are guilty of customizing dinnertime. But it's a treat, not the norm. Most nights, I make one meal. This particular night, it was kale and quinoa salad with chicken. And Jack let us know he wasn't having it.

"Fine!" he said in a huff. "Then I'll just run away!"

I let out a laugh with the context of, "Oh, really now—is that so?" and he shook his head yes. That tugged at my feelings, of course. As a mom I do everything I can to show my love. I make the boys a warm breakfast before school every day, I put notes in their lunch boxes, and just try to stop me from grinning when I pick them up from school—and now Jack wants to run away because he "has" to eat the dinner I made him?

"Well, Jack, that sure makes me sad," I said. "We're going to miss you." I run to his room, snag his suitcase and teddy bear, and then go back to the kitchen to pack him a lunch.

He watched in silence.

As I sliced the bread and slid it into a baggie, I asked, "Have you thought about where you'll run to?"

He didn't respond. I looked over. His lip was quivering.

"To you, Mommy." He threw his arms around my hips. "I only want you—I'm sorry." That night, Jack inhaled a plate of quinoa and chicken. Today it stands as his favorite meal.

no. 4: demonstrate the power of the universe

I'm big on nature. I don't know how to say this any other way—I love the sky and the stars and the way the moon hangs in the air. Many days and nights, I remind the boys to look up, check out the clouds, take in the sunrise, and look at the moon. I love the moon. Just think—if the moon came out only once a year, everyone on Earth would stop and celebrate this big white thing in the sky. But we all take the moon for granted. We rush around, focused on getting where we need to be, not even noticing the moon most of the time. I think recognizing the moon and its enormity gives you perspective. To think about how small we are is humbling and a little intimidating. Just the lesson I want to give to my kids.

One evening about a year ago, I was fast asleep when I felt a tap on my shoulder.

"Mom," Carson whispered, "wake up."

Ugh. I thought. *He's sick.*

"I'm sorry to wake you, but you have to get up and follow me."

Worried, I got out of bed and stumbled behind him. We turned the corner to his room, and he pointed at the window. "Look at the moon, Mom. Isn't it amazing tonight?"

"Oh, man! Yes, it is!" But honestly, all I could really think was *no, Carson, you are.*

no. 5: praise acts of kindness

Giving it back, paying it forward, the Golden Rule, whatever you call acts of kindness, I believe that demonstrating goodness toward others is essential for every child to understand and act upon.

One day when Carson was in first grade, he packed an extra pair of socks in his backpack. I figured he needed a backup for recess or PE. I wasn't sure why he couldn't just wear the pair he had on but assumed he must have a reason.

"I just want an extra pair," he said nonchalantly. So I left it at that.

Later that week, I got my answer. Carson explained that his friend got in trouble for not wearing socks two days in a row. The friend told him he didn't have any that fit him, so Carson took it on himself to make sure he was taken care of. I don't think I've ever been so proud of him. Having such a good heart at that young age is better than straight As on every report card. That night, his dad tucked him in bed and told him a similar story from when he was a child—but it was reversed. I've seen my husband cry only a few times, and this was one of them.

To this day, we make it a point to buy a coffee for the person behind us in Starbucks. We pick up groceries for others, including some of the elderly in our neighborhood. On those occasions, I have the boys join me because I want them to see the importance of kindness. This is the same way my grandmother taught me when I was a child.

no. 6: showcase and record their whimsy

In 2010, I started a Facebook page called Garrett Brothers—Kid Critics, Inc. It's a place where I post videos of Carson and Jack reviewing classic kids' movies like *Despicable Me, Marmaduke, Turbo, Shrek, Free Birds,* and so on. There are tons of giggles, lots of plot spoilers, and plenty of very important opinions of what works and doesn't work for these budding movie *aficionados*. Not only does this Facebook page provide a digital scrapbook, it's a place where they can be creative, funny, and irreverent. Technology allows us to create our own cyber footprints of certain moments in time that will last long into the future. And won't it be a blast to view these videos in ten, fifteen, or twenty years to see what then-four-year-old Jack and then-nine-year-old Carson thought of *Toy Story 3*? Here's a hint: My mini critics thought it was just "an OK movie"—two out of four thumbs up. However, Carson admitted to falling asleep, so perhaps this particular review was a bit harsh.

no. 7: establish traditions

Every summer for the past four years, we purchase an enormous canvas from an art store; the boys have to pick three things important to them that year, and they take turns painting it until we have a finished product. Each year, I document what the things are on the back of the canvas because often an explanation is needed to decipher what exactly they've drawn. Some examples include: the Wiggles, Pokémon, LEGOs, *Call of Duty*, and FC Dallas. We do this for three reasons.

1. We want to establish a fun family tradition that also serves as a journal for the stage where our kids are in life as evidenced by their interests for that given year. How fun will it be for Jack to remember at age thirty that he loved Elmo when he was four years old?

2. We want our kids to take the time to realize how lucky they are to have had the things or experiences from the year.

3. We think this is a great way for our kids to take stock of what they have—to be critical thinkers and understand that a year has passed, they have grown, and they've had experiences that make them who they are.

In 2012, the boys went about painting their canvas. Jack drew a stick figure.

"Cute!" I said. "Mickey Mouse? Diego?" As I said before, sometimes it's hard to tell exactly what they're drawing.

Jack leaned in, as if he were sharing a big secret, "It's Carson. He's important to me."

Carson looked up, and without a word, he walked over and hugged his little brother.

That moment was reason enough to keep our canvas-drawing tradition alive for the next one hundred years. If I were to draw what's important to me, I'd draw my boys together, hugging or playing ball—something that demonstrated them loving each other. Our annual drawings help my husband and me remember and document as well. We are lucky to have our children—and we're even luckier they recognize each other's value.

"You're the only brothers you'll ever have," I've advised after a fight or snarky exchange. "You better be nice to each other."

And guess what? In the moment when Jack drew Carson, I knew my message had been heard loud and clear.

5

the a-team

*Report cards aren't tarot cards. You want
to know what foretells the future? The way
you help to build your child's character.*

I f my reports cards told the future, I was destined for
a job as a road-kill cleaner. This is the reason I don't
believe that report cards or grades, in general, necessarily provide a forecast of adult skill, ambition, or success. Or, most importantly, predict a person's character.

When I was in grade school, middle school, and
high school, no one ever asked once to see my report
card. My grandma didn't ever think I should be in
school, let alone care whether or not I was mastering
the material. And trust me, I wasn't.

I specifically remember a day in sixth grade when I
woke my grandma so she could drive me to school. As

I've explained before, she worked late in a bar, and she liked to get her drink on. These facts don't translate into a happy mood at 7:00 a.m. when an enthusiastic little girl announces she's ready to begin her day—I was a disruption to her routine.

Memaw was mad and tired and confused. "Why do you need school?" she barked at me. "No one else in our family needed school." She was referring to herself, of course, and to her own children who redefined truancy.

Of course, at age eleven, I didn't have a response beyond tears. I just knew I liked school. I liked my friends, PE, recess, and lunchtime. In school, I had a place. I had a safe haven. I had comfort. I made my way in school through all of the cliques and fit in with everyone. Social interactions were fun for me. My friends and schoolmates were my family. Even after school, I'd go home with my friends. And thank goodness I had the opportunity to do so. It was my friends' families who gave me structure and familiarity. If it weren't for them, I would've been screwed.

Children need a dose of discipline. Boundaries are important to help define the world. At home with Memaw, I didn't have so much as one line drawn in the sand. And as I got older, my need for discipline grew. Around 1978, my dad resurfaced. Gone were his crazy days, he was a new man—a born-again Christian—and he was ready to make up for lost time. He fought hard to get me every other weekend; my grandmother was not happy about this—she fought back, but in the end, I think she even recognized the need for him in my life. He had remarried a wonderful woman, and to this day, they are happily married. She changed him for the better, and I am so thankful for that. Most significantly, he wanted me in his life. So I began seeing my dad every other weekend. They were dirt poor, but they both worked hard to provide a different life when my weekend arrived. Again, it was not something I recognized as a child, but as an adult, I look back and see it with eyes wide open.

If you want to know how I define polar opposites, let me explain what it was like to live with my dad on the weekends in contrast to the way I was used to things being.

Dad's house: Not allowed to watch *Three's Company*. My alternate "entertainment" included folding clothes and cleaning the toilets.

Memaw's house: I fell asleep watching *MTV*. There was always a pile of dirty clothes to dig through for tomorrow's outfit. And as for the toilets, please don't get me started.

Dad's house: Bed by 8:00 p.m.

Memaw's house: Bed by 8:00 a.m. if you feel like it.

Dad's house: Conversation with my stepmom about the birds and the bees.

Memaw's house: Learned about sex by watching strangers have sex in our pool. Often.

Dad's house: No cursing. Ever.

Memaw's house: No sentence was complete without a four-letter word.

Dad's house: Dinner was at 6:00 p.m. Your hands better be washed, and you better bring your manners.

Memaw's house: Eat if you're hungry; there's a can of tuna in the pantry.

The contrast between life at my dad's house and life at Memaw's taught me what I'd come to see as the value and irony of juxtaposition. I think the experience of each jolting reality helped to lay the foundation for my ability to adapt. At Dad's house, I had to act like a good girl—an obedient, church-going, rule-following sweetheart who loved her daddy and the Lord. At Memaw's house, all hell could break loose, and no one would notice, unless I accidently put a hole through the roof when it was raining. I became who I needed to become in each scenario. I rose to the occasion and situation put before me. I think this back-and-forth life helped me learn to listen, assess, and then act. I think it was one of the reasons I did so well in the business world. I knew the best strategy at home—whichever home I was in—was to shush and listen. That belief translated into the boardroom as well. My success as an adult had nothing to do with whether or not I passed the history class pop quiz. Spoiler: I didn't.

Classes and science fair projects and grades have an important place. But if your child isn't on the path for class valedictorian, isn't that OK too?

As for our family, our boys are very different. They are worlds apart really. Here's how I see the breakdown for each of my boys and how I help to enrich their individual styles.

Carson: He's motivated by positive feedback. He does the very best in classes where the teachers provide support and reach out when they see things slipping. He craves structure, although he'd never verbally admit it. We help to build his confidence through his participation in soccer, basketball, and football. He's that kid who's humble and polite, the one always wearing a smile. He's an animal lover, opens doors for elders and women, and says "thank you" and "please."

Poignant moment for Mom: We had the television on during a political debate that, at one particular point, got heated. A few moments later, we all piled into the car for dinner out, and as we buckled in, Carson said, "Wouldn't it be great if aliens came down and attacked us? Then we would all—as humans—have to stick together to defend our planet instead of fighting each other over stupid stuff." He was ten years old. Although it was such a pie-in-the-sky, little-boy thing to say, I thought that small sentiment was brilliant. I still do.

Jack: He's motivated by attention. He does the very best when everyone's watching. And if no one's paying attention, he'll make sure to change that. Since he's in the second grade, grades are hard to define. He's not into sports like Carson; he cooks, writes stories, and draws. Every night before bed, he asks, "Just ten more minutes to play imagination. Tonight I'm an astronaut."

Poignant moment for Mom: On New Year's Eve when we sit down for dinner, we share our resolutions. At age six, Jack's resolution was to get to know other cultures, including the foods and languages, so he could understand people around the world better. I was amazed that his resolution wasn't to get the latest set of LEGOs or to win a million billion dollars. Nope, it was "To get to know the world," as he put it.

The point of illustrating the differences between these two boys is to explain that there are inevitable, necessary differences for each child. As parents, we have to adapt our strategies, lessons, ideas, and expectations—academic and otherwise—for each child. Not every child can come in first place. And no matter how different your kids are from each other—and from the others in your neighborhood or school—there will always be those "stop-and-listen" moments that touch your soul.

Last year, I noticed that while Jack had begun to take responsibility for creating his own schedule, setting up his alarm on his own, and even using a planner to keep track of whatever it is a seven-year-old needs to keep track of, I also noticed that he acted uninspired by school. He needed a more creative environment. At that time both boys were in a private Catholic school, and this great school is ideal for a child needing a set agenda with structure like Carson, but it wasn't ideal for a self-paced child like Jack. So we kept Carson in the Catholic school and moved Jack to a Montessori school, which is founded on the idea that each child moves at his or her own pace and the lessons and curriculum can be adjusted to each child's needs. We adapted our strategies to fit the child. Today both kids are thriving in their respective environments.

the value of teachers

No one expected me to be a Rhodes Scholar, but schools enforce extracurricular restrictions if you don't at least demonstrate a baseline understanding of the core subject matter. This is precisely why the "no-pass, no-play" rule was put into effect. In grade school, the rule didn't apply. But it was a whole new game in high school. If I wanted to do anything—even be a member of the knitting club—I had to have passing grades. In other words, you couldn't gobble up the cupcake until you ate your broccoli first.

When I look back, I see now how vital the role of teachers was to my well-being. My survival. There were teachers and counselors who stepped in to help at opportune times. Although I didn't recognize it then, I do now. Every day, when I drop my boys off for school, I know they're lucky to have opportunities to learn outside the textbooks. They get to learn from their teachers. Therefore, it blows my mind why we undervalue educators. There have been many articles, op-eds, and pundits sounding off on how teachers are the most undervalued professionals in the world. And I agree.

When I was in school, several teachers asked me, "What's going on at home?" I'm sure there were many conversations in the background about keeping an eye out for me. Their concern wasn't about my grades—they didn't think a little TLC would get me on the honor roll. There were too many other things in my life that needed to be fixed. Their concern was for me as a person, a healthy teenager, a future woman. I got help far and near from a handful of teachers. They made sure I passed my classes, so I could take advantage of social opportunities because they recognized that those situations were what really kept me going. I couldn't run for homecoming queen if I didn't pass my classes. I couldn't be on student council unless I passed my classes. I couldn't be on the tennis team or play any other sport without passing my classes.

So I did what was necessary to get by in my studies, and then I blew it out of the water to achieve citizenship and social successes.

I was vice president of the student council from 1988–89, on the tennis team from 1988–89, and crowned homecoming queen in 1988. The day after I was crowned, as I was sprawled across my bed reading an old copy of *Seventeen*, Memaw walked in, leaned against the door, and waited for me to look up. "Linda just called and said you made homecoming queen last night."

I nodded. I hadn't said a word to anyone in my family about being nominated. I even walked by myself to a store that had a dress I could afford, bought it four sizes too big because that's all they had, and made it work. I did my own hair and makeup and figured out on my own how I should wear the wrist corsage. I had no connection to Memaw outside of the house, and it was OK. I'd quit making any effort to communicate, and no one even noticed. I wasn't doing drugs or getting into trouble. I was just doing my own thing. And not having anyone at home notice was really OK because the night before, as I stood as homecoming queen before my entire class, the football team, and a stadium filled with spectators, I heard enough applause and cheers to know that I mattered.

And not one single person had a clue that, according to the Iowa Tests of Basic Skills, I scored 4 out of 100 in math. And this meant that I scored lower than 96 percent of the rest of the children—in the entire country.

6

alone again, naturally

*Being by yourself isn't the same as being
alone. True solitude allows you to get
inside your own head.*

Self-esteem is complicated. A person who has a
healthy dose of it can come across the wrong
way. A person who has an anemic dose can
come across the wrong way. So what's the right way?
Self-esteem isn't a teachable skill like good manners
or great cooking. It develops through pattern, experience, interpretation, and belief. I don't mean to
sound philosophical—I just want to explain where
I'm coming from before I dive in to the importance of
leveraging all available tools to help foster self-esteem
in others. I believe that contented children make for
contented adults. And if you look across the table in

the boardroom, in the PTA meeting, on the school bus, in the mall, or wherever your professional and personal life takes you, I bet you see plenty of people who could've used an esteem boost when they were kids. Ultimately self-esteem is a private, individual matter. But, as I see it, parents are the conduit.

As I look back at my life, I can point to many instances where adversity taught me to believe in myself. I can point to successes that taught me self-confidence. I can point to decisions that I made where I learned to accept my abilities and limitations. So how do I help my children drive on the road to stable self-esteem? Sometimes that means letting go of the reins.

wired to survive

Carson is a smart boy. He is a capable child with great potential. In school, he gets good grades in most of his classes. Note that I said most but not all. Now as his mom I want nothing more than to swoop in and rescue him—help him get those As. But he has to realize he's Carson Garrett, and it's his responsibility to work hard, work smart, and reach his potential. I'm just his mom. He'll either rise above or get chewed up.

So I want him to learn now—when he's old enough to understand the difference—that I'm here for him no matter what, that I love and support him no matter what, but that there are situations where he has to take control, work hard, and do what it takes.

We want Carson to figure out that he must study, do his homework, and absorb the material or he won't pass. If he falls short of those requirements, he'll be disappointed, and if the grade is poor enough, he won't be able to play sports at school. We believe that a less-than-stellar grade would fuel his desire to put more energy into making sure it doesn't happen again. So this is the reason we step back and let him learn that lesson. And when he does learn from it, he's building upon the foundation for healthy self-esteem.

For example, I recently received an e-mail from one of Carson's teachers alerting me to the fact that he wasn't doing so great in one of his classes. I appreciated very much her attention to his situation and her desire to immediately connect through e-mail. As I crafted my reply, I was nervous. I didn't want to sound callous or uninterested in Carson's grades, but I wanted her to understand why I was going to choose to stay on the sidelines.

I wrote back to the teacher that I was going to let Carson figure things out for himself—the sink-or-swim sort of thing. I explained to her that Carson was the type of young person who needed to learn by doing, and that he was the student, not me, and as such, he knew what was required to get the grade. I explained that I was confident in his ability to recognize what was expected of him and that he might just have to get a bad grade to push himself harder to reach his potential. I also told her how hard it was to not rescue Carson. The teacher wrote back and said she found my stand refreshing and honest. She also said she wished more parents thought as we did.

Maybe more parents do think as we do but don't know that it's OK to step aside for longer-term good. I just remind myself of the fact that humans are wired to survive. It's our nature to do what it takes to ensure our own longevity. If we step aside at opportune moments, we can teach our kids to dig deep, persevere, and prosper.

the value of being alone

There's great value in spending time alone. Personally some of my greatest lessons and tests came from those times when I was quiet and alone. There's a difference between being alone physically and then being alone mentally. I was often alone as a child. Being by myself had some advantages, but there were also many lonely moments. I held conversations daily with the moon and sun, and I really believed they were listening, plus they seemed a little lonely too. There was something peaceful and comforting about looking up and seeing these enormous glowing beautiful objects that seemed to hang in the sky. They were consistently there anytime I looked up. (You know you're alone way too much if your closest friends live in space.) I think the fact I developed—by force—a deep sense of self-reliance was why middle school and high school drama really didn't affect me. If I sensed it was coming on, I just retreated to my own environment. I had plenty of friends and interactions, but I would evade conflict or gossip at any turn. Unfortunately sometimes my own environment wasn't the best place for me.

I remember Fourth of July—I was in seventh grade—and things were crazy at the house. Drugs, people partying out of control, and my need to get out. I was in the way. So on that Fourth of July, I filled my backpack and left. The music was so loud that no one heard the front door slam.

In the dark, I made my way to a bridge that went over Interstate 30. The city's fireworks show had just begun, and as I walked way above the traffic, I turned to watch. The intense colors were glorious. And in that moment, I specifically remember knowing, somehow, that it was utterly unnatural for an eleven-year-old girl to be on a bridge at night alone. I remember thinking, *I don't want to be this person.* And even though I had no parental guidance or supervision, I knew that smoking pot and drinking before school and sleeping under a pile of blankets to drown out the sounds of rock music blasting at midnight were not normal situations. I cried standing on the bridge. But that night, all alone, I promised the moon and God that I was ready to make a change. As soon as I declared it, I felt a sense of self-pride. Had I not been alone mentally, I don't know that I would've had the opportunity to stop, realize, and react.

I composed myself and walked to my best friend Kara's house. I stayed there for a few days. Kara's mom was nurturing and loving. In that environment, I liked who I was. The emotion was so strong that I knew I wouldn't let anyone make me feel as if I needed to do something or be someone else to fit in. That was my turning point.

Because I was alone—physically and mentally—I believe I was able to talk with myself and make a change. I think most people, myself included, learn from those impossibly difficult situations—divorce, layoffs, illness—and if we force ourselves to take the time to stop when we're smack in the middle of the ugliness, there's often a self-building component.

being alone to regroup or grow up

As an adult, alone time is hard to find. There's work, friends, kids, and your spouse all vying for your attention. Sometimes alone time is relegated to a few seconds in the bathroom. But there's this interesting irony that happens when you're a mom: you crave alone time, beg for it, and then, when you finally get it, you miss your kids. There's rarely a moment without guilt or feeling the strong need to make a peanut butter-and-jelly sandwich or help tie a shoe. As a mom, I have to force myself to look away from those heart-tugging emotions and go for a run, take a surf lesson alone when traveling to the coast, or simply drive the long way home listening to a good song—one that brings back a happy memory. I've also found that practicing yoga gives me the chance to get inside my own head, and most of the time I forget that there's anyone else in the room. It's just me and my thoughts, even though my thoughts are normally, "God, I hate my boobs" or "Man, I need a pedicure—my toes look like Shrek's."

Usually when I spend time alone to think or to not think, I come back into my "real" life in a better emotional place. I feel stronger. My self-esteem feels fed.

But even if you do get time to be quiet and alone, there's another great interrupter to be wary of. Technology tempts us to be perpetually connected to others. It's hard to turn off the computers, smart-phones, and video games and just hang out with a puzzle or a journal. I think most of us want to pace like confined wild cats when we are without our gadgets.

I see the way technology robs us of being alone, and it invades our sense of self-reliance. I'm as guilty as anyone, telling myself I need to have my phone so I can take a picture or record a moment. But more often than not, I'm online.

As Carson grows up, we've noticed he's often by himself, but he's never alone. If there isn't another person around, he's with his Nintendo DS, computer, iPad, or smartphone. His alone time is attached to fantasy. So we made a rule in our house—technology-free weekends. The first tech-free weekend, we went to the ranch. Carson spent hours outside digging in the clay, feeding the cows, and riding the tractor with his dad. I saw a reincarnation of that young adventurer I so missed. He never once asked for his electronics. He acted happier and like a boy—not a silent robot thinking of a way to build his next farm in *Minecraft*.

For Jack, alone time is completely different. He wants to be by himself so he can "play imagination." Most nights before bed, I'll find him in his room being someone different: a unicorn tamer, a lawnmower man, a kung fu fighter. This alone time gives him validation because his fantasies are all created by him. And by the time I've tucked him in, he actually believes that he could fight the best kung fu fighter, tame a unicorn, and mow the lawn. There's incredible joy in that!

what's a woman to do?

Today I'm not rushing around to important work meetings or pulling all-nighters to get a presentation complete. Today I don't stress about suits at the cleaners or a broken briefcase strap or finding time to drink my coffee before answering a barrage of e-mails. The absence of a high-pressure, consuming career means there's time to do other things. Which sounds good. Feels good. Is good. But it'll be even better when I figure out who I am in this stage of my life.

Self-esteem is an animal that needs constant feeding. Just as our children are defined in part by how we raise them, we are defined in part by how we raise our kids. But when the kids are in school, and I realize it's just me and the TV, it's time to reinvent myself. I take cooking lessons, golf lessons, and yoga so I can try new things, go new places, and meet new people. I hang out with old friends and revisit old haunts to remember the past. I'm searching for the next big thing for myself. I want to discover what makes me interesting. When I find those qualities, I'll go whole hog nurturing them, just as I do for my kids, and just as I hope they do for themselves.

7

like a fine wine

Older people have been there, done that.
There's some comfort in realizing that they
totally know you're about to screw up.

My memaw once said, "When you're finally comfortable in your own skin, it's wrinkled." I've often wondered why this is the case. It seems that when we're younger, we make a lot of silly assumptions about ourselves, our abilities, and even our purpose, and if we just had the privilege of foresight, we'd certainly be spared much heartache and dumb mistakes. But I guess that's the point—to have to go through many things to get to the place you should be. As a parent, it's difficult to watch your kids stumble. But sometimes stepping back is the best thing you could ever do. In my own childhood, I often wished someone would step up, but if anyone had—my mother, my relatives, or in the early days, my father—I'd be different than I am now. So, in the end, I guess it all worked out.

In her own way and to the best of her ability, my grandma was my guidepost. Even today, I think that my grandma, in spite of all of her faults, is the wisest person I know. She'll cuss up and down until your ears bleed, but then she has this delicate appreciation for life. She'd drink herself into a fuzzy stupor until 5:00 a.m. and then wake me up by throwing open the curtains and announcing, "It's September 3, 1984, Kimberly, and there's only ONE September 3, 1984. Don't you waste it! Get out of bed and start your day!"

Isn't it funny how often irony enters our lives?

Memaw goes against the grain of what you'd associate with a "grandma." There were no homemade chocolate chip cookies, no braids for my hair, no birthday presents, no Christmas trees, and certainly no puzzle games, coloring, or teatime with the dollies. There were zero boo-boo kisses, no special trips to the ice cream parlor, and no pizza dinners for good grades (not that I actually got good grades). My grandma's everyday approach to raising me was utilitarian: she was my guardian because there was no other viable option. She's as tough as an old, worn boot but has a heart of gold. Her wisdom came from decades of elbow grease and sweat equity, of barkeeping, and of making ends meet. There wasn't a drink she could resist or a cigarette that wasn't her friend. But she was there for me—albeit in her own way.

I think parents—and all adults—are wise to at least listen to the advice of their elders, even if they think they're too old, out of touch, or living in a different world in a social or economic context. I also think listening—and paying attention—to things you don't agree with, or patterns and behaviors you don't want to emulate—can help you make the right choices too.

If we, as parents and adults, don't listen to those who have been there before, then really, we're no different from the kids, 'tweens, and teens we're trying to raise ourselves. Cue the eye rolls now as I share some of the advice I was given—and actually listened to.

remember your ice (in case of emergency)

When I was seven years old, my aunt and I hitchhiked to a lake about an hour away to meet up with my mom and her friends. I'm sure I was an afterthought. My guess is that my aunt was looking after me and couldn't resist the invitation to party, so she just included me because there was nowhere else I could go.

As I walked along the dusty road in the direction of the lake with my aunt facing ongoing traffic, her thumb pointed out in the familiar "I-need-a-lift" sign. I remember being aware that my grandma wouldn't approve and would've screamed at us for doing something like this. But as a seven year old, no one was going to listen to me protest, especially not my aunt who was hell-bent on having a good time. So after we had been walking along for a while, a dirty black Toyota pulled up alongside us. A man talked to us through the window, inviting us to get in. I crawled into the backseat; my aunt took the front.

I saw my aunt checking out the driver who had this quietly weird vibe. He seemed creepy, but then again, anyone who picks up hitchhikers isn't exactly a poster child for normalcy. I remember that my aunt asked him to drop us off before we actually got to the lake. I think she was afraid. I saw how tightly she was holding on to the side of the seat, so I guess she was nervous. The driver pulled over, and we got out, and as we walked away, he sat in his car watching. I was practically running to keep up with my aunt as she charged down the side of the road. We wound up walking for what seemed like forever to reach the lake.

When we got to the lake, my mom cheered and ran up to my aunt, throwing her arms around her shoulders. She didn't even look at me. I knew instantly that my mom was drunk or high. There were about a dozen adults there; everyone was laughing, yelling, and partying. I remember feeling sleepy and lying down on this abandoned mattress that had been tossed out onto the sand.

I woke up about four hours later and looked around. Everyone had left. Not a soul in sight. I was terrified. I called out. No answer. I was so sunburned it hurt to stand up. My skin felt like it was covered with angry sunshine. I started crying and calling out for my aunt. I walked in the direction of the parking lot in search of a pay phone.

Memaw had taught me to memorize the phone number to the Beer Pump, my ICE (in case of emergency), and told me to call her collect if I ever needed her. She showed me how to do it over and over until I understood. Through tears, I saw a pay phone in the parking lot. Remembering the steps Memaw outlined, I made a collect call to the bar. She answered, and after she accepted the call, I told her through anxious gasps that everyone had left, and I was alone at the lake, which I thought was Lake Benbrook. I guess Memaw deduced that was the only lake around, and she sent someone from the bar to pick me up.

As I sat there shaking because I was so burned, I was at once hurt and angry to the core. And even though I was only seven years old, I remember that day very well. I couldn't believe my aunt, her friends, and my own mother could just leave me. No one had the sense to slather me with sunscreen. No one cared if I'd eaten or had water. And not a soul even bothered to wonder how I'd get home.

Now with kids of my own, I can't imagine what was going through their minds. My mother had no accountability for me—a person she made from her own body. But here's one thing I'm certain of—my mom didn't completely forget me. I believe she pretended to forget me, probably blamed the absence of thought on the drugs, but I know that she was cognizant that I was left behind. I think she secretly wished something would happen to me. If something bad happened to me, it would dissolve her of her burden of having a child. All she wanted was to party and be free of responsibility. With me gone, her real desires could come true.

That day, two things became clear to me: My mother would passively do just about anything to lose me, and no matter what happened to me, my Memaw was always just a collect call away. As simple as that sounds, having a line to Memaw was a hundred times better than lying in the scorching sun on an abandoned mattress.

choose your friends and your allies wisely

I was in second grade when the schools changed their admissions and began bussing students to different classes in an effort to mix up the neighborhoods. My new school was close to what we called the projects or government-subsidized housing. I wasn't aware at that time what the projects were or what the social and economic implications were. Then I was just more disappointed it was going to be a longer bus ride to get to school and that I would not get to play with my friends at recess. But Memaw knew I was entering rocky territory. So that morning, after I'd put on my favorite green corduroys and came into the kitchen for a bowl of cereal, Memaw pulled up one of her wooden dining chairs and leaned in. She slid a Snickers bar across the table.

"Kimberly Zane." When she used my middle name, as all kids know, that meant business, "I want you to find the biggest and meanest kid at the school. I want you to walk up to him and introduce yourself. Then give him this candy bar."

"Why?" Honestly I asked because I wanted to eat it myself. A Snickers bar was a way better breakfast than cornflakes.

"Just do it," was all Memaw said.

So I did. As I walked the halls of my new school, I saw familiar faces and a few friends from my previous school, but the whole vibe was different. I saw a tall, angry-faced, lonely looking boy standing by the stairs. I went up to him, introduced myself, and gave him the candy bar. That kid was my instant friend. And no one at the school ever messed with me once. Memaw's advice, for all its simplicity, was packed with street smarts.

never shy away from hard work

If I lost all of my finances tomorrow, you bet I'd do whatever it took to ensure my family was taken care of. I know the importance of hard work. I think most of my generation understands that it could take having two jobs—even three—at once to get where you wanted to be. I've never thought any job was beneath me, and I've had plenty of paying-the-dues moments. I'll never forget about a moment of clarity that came in my mid-twenties. I was working for the Dallas Cowboys in a job I loved as an administrative assistant, and I asked my boss for a raise. Guess what he told me?

"If you need more money, get a second job."

I wasn't offended in the least. So I got a job at night waiting tables. It was perfectly fine, and I considered it a rite of passage. I never once thought I was above waiting tables or working long hours. It was what I needed to do to get by. So I did.

My dad is a perfect example of someone with a solid work ethic. In the nineties, he'd been working for a Christian publisher and got laid off. He was living in Colorado Springs at the time, and the job market wasn't great. So guess what he did? He took a job as a customer service associate at a Levi's retail store. Retail! He was rubbing elbows with teenagers who were making the same hourly rate he was. But he did what he had to do while he tried to figure out the next step. And then came his moment of clarity. He decided to pursue what he had always desired to do and became a preacher. With no college or seminary training, he studied for the exams necessary to be ordained as a preacher in the Presbyterian Church of America. And had my dad not gotten knocked down by losing his publishing job, he might not ever have had the courage—or push—to take a different path.

There are instances in my life that were horrible, but I also consider those to be lessons. By watching some of the actions of my grandmother and all of the actions of my mother, I knew what I didn't want to become. In this sense, I got advice for sure but not in the way they intended. By seeing who they were, watching how they behaved, and feeling the brunt of their poor choices, I learned to define myself by what I was not.

This is not necessarily an observation I hope anyone reading this book had to experience. But if you were in undesirable situations or places, it's my hope that you can harness the wisdom and turn it into your favor.

When I was older, middle school age, I was aware of how late my grandma and grandpa got home after the bar closed. I usually fell asleep with the television on, but even when they stumbled in at two thirty in the morning, they argued so loudly that the noise always trumped the TV, and I'd wake up. There were also occasions when the yelling escalated into throwing—dishes, shoes, anything within reach—and then physical tussles. The police were at the house a few times in those instances. But each morning after, I'd emerge from my room and do my best to act nonchalant, and Memaw did the same. She always behaved as if everything was A-OK. After all, my grandparents weren't exactly traditional. They never even slept in their bed—every evening they crashed on the couches in the living room with the TV on.

Looking back, I think those years may have been the hardest for Memaw. She worked like a dog until the wee hours, drank every day, and then had the extra responsibility of me. I know that in that entire mix, I was the anomaly. Why was I there? What was my purpose? Memaw didn't understand why I even bothered to go to school. To her, life experience was where the true education lay. But every day, I guess out of obligation, or maybe not wanting to babysit me, she'd pull herself up off the couch, push back her disheveled hair, and get in her car to drive me to school. There were plenty of days she was still drunk. And there were those days when the alcohol got the better of her, and she'd just yell at me out of frustration.

"Why the hell do you need to even go to this damn school? Just quit and get to work!"

I'd respond by keeping my gaze out the passenger window. In those moments, it didn't occur to her that I was only twelve years old.

In high school, I blossomed. I found my voice so to speak. I had great friends, played on the tennis team, and made the drill team. I was hardly ever home, by choice, and nobody noticed unless it suited them. My mother would randomly show up when she wanted to exert her authority or demonstrate her inherent right to control me since she was "my mother." It usually happened when she needed something. Once my friend Lara had a party during the summer. As we all hung out watching *Dirty Dancing*, the doorbell rang. It was my mother. I guess Memaw told her where I was. Anyway, she was at the front door, totally fried on some drug, and yelling at me to get in the car. I did what she commanded, I guess, because I was worried something was wrong. I'd seen her only once in the entire year.

"I'm going to Eckerd's," she announced as she weaved down the streets. "I want to get you something. You want some Lee Press-on nails?" Eckerd's was a drugstore chain—think CVS or Walgreens—that's no longer in business. There was no hug. No "How are you, honey?" No nothing but Lee Press-on nails. Seriously.

"Sure," I said to avoid conflict. We drove the rest of the way not talking. She pulled into the Eckerd's parking lot and got out of the car. I'm not sure why she wanted me to stay behind, but I did as I was told.

I waited thirty minutes, and then I heard the thump of someone tapping on the window. It was a police officer.

"Ma'am, your mom is heading to jail. Do you have a driver's license?"

I took a moment to process. *Had she tried to steal the fake nails? How could she get in trouble in Eckerd's?*

I rummaged through my purse and pulled out my wallet. "Yes, officer," I said and held up my license.

I sat right where I was watching the cops haul my mother off to jail. I got into the driver's side and drove the car back to Memaw's house. Then I called Lara and asked her to come pick me up. I never told anyone what happened. Lara knew not to ask. To this day, I have no idea what my mother wanted or what happened. I just knew that I never understood her behavior. The randomness of her encounters did nothing but make me sad. Sad for her because I was never going to be anything like the woman she chose to be.

pay attention to sweetness

As I've said before, I believe the greatest decision you'll ever make is whom you choose to marry. For me personally, my turning point in life was meeting my husband. His support is immeasurable. But it's the small and often quiet actions that remind me of the kind-hearted man he is.

When Danny and I were in the dating phase, we did some stupid things, including break up. The reason we broke up was that I was ready for marriage early, but he wasn't. I knew Danny was the one, but he had a plan, like always (he's a list maker), and his plan was to marry at thirty. Well, we were twenty-two, and there was no way I was waiting eight years. So I broke up with him. I cursed his dumb plan. Oh how I hated how precise he was with his list making and detailed outlines. Isn't it funny how the things that attract you to your partner, the things you know that balance you out, the things that you need, can be—and usually are—the things that drive you crazy? A couple of weeks later, I saw Danny. The stress and sadness of the breakup made him a mess. He'd lost twenty pounds, his eyes looked tiny behind the puffy bags, and he projected this sad and despondent vibe. We were both depressed about being apart, so after a long talk, we decided to give it another go. There's nothing like a little time apart to create perspective.

The following week we visited my dad and stepmom at their house on Lake Granbury. My dad had a speedboat, and with Danny at the wheel, we set out for an afternoon of tubing and waterskiing. As Danny cruised the lake, I was doing my best to stay on the inner tube, but at one turn, I fell off. I attempted to pull myself back up and over the black rubber but had no luck. Danny watched me struggle a few times and then turned the boat off and dove in. He grabbed hold of my legs, gave my booty a push, and in a moment, I was back inside the tube. My hero, right?

We drove back to the dock, me riding the tube like Miss America on parade. As Danny tied the boat up and I toweled off, my dad pulled me aside. With his eyes on my boyfriend, he leaned in and shared his observation: "Now that's the kind of guy you want to marry."

I watched Danny tie a flawless knot and then pull the cooler out of the boat. And as he walked up the dock and back to the house, I knew that what my dad had seen was absolutely spot-on correct.

listen to yourself

At the end of the day, the person responsible for you is you. The person who can succumb to adversity, fall into the middle of controversy, and triumph over difficulty is you. Your own drive, desires, focus, and moxie determine more than circumstances. I, for one, wouldn't change a thing about my past—not even the stuff that still to this day makes my stomach hurt. What I try to do is take everything I know and everything I believe in from others and use it all to help my kids find their way. I do my part. But they are young humans. They too will grow up to listen to their own instincts, navigate their own way, and be who they want to be.

I remind myself regularly to listen to what I know. I too am an elder—a person of much wisdom. I have to take time to talk to myself. I remind myself to sit quietly and reflect on what I've experienced. I listen to others, and I certainly follow advice. (Thank you, Dad, for pointing out what I really did know to be true about Danny that day on the lake.) But I also believe that everything we do is couched in the context of who we are in all moments—the good, the bad, and the ugly.

It's up to us to remember we can leverage all of what we know by listening to our own voices.

8

balancing act

The key to happiness is balance. The best lesson ever is learning its value.

Every day we strive for balance. If you're a working parent, you know the struggle between office time and family time. If you're a parent of school-aged kids, you know the struggle between good grades and extracurricular activities. If you're a human being, you know the struggle between eating right and eating fun, going out and staying in, sleeping enough and getting things done. I could go on and on.

Whatever roles you fulfill, there exists a counteraction that will test your resolve, make you work harder, or just give you a healthy dose of conflict. As such, we're all consistently chasing balance because that's where life works. When your family is taken care of, when your career needs are met, when your finances are in order, when you've made time to exercise, when your body is working in harmony, and overall, you feel like you've got it together. It's when you can let out that contented sigh, plop onto the couch, turn on a movie, sip a glass of Cabernet, and feel a sense of peace. But is it balance?

Perhaps it is for the moment, but at any point something or someone can push you off center. This is the reason I believe that the quest to achieve balance is this never-ending, vital, delicately frustrating goal. You can have those reflective calming moments, but you can't have forever. And just when you think you've got it all figured out, when work and home and friends and personal fulfillment all have their respective piece of the pie, you can easily get knocked off course. It's like striving for perfection. It exists in concept, but most of the time it's just ever so slightly out of reach. I think balance is designed to be this way so that you never become complacent, and you never stop trying. Or maybe it's like the Loch Ness Monster. People claim to know it exists, but the majority of people have never seen proof.

All of this talk about the quest for balance can't happen unless you've established a strong foundation from which to work.

- You have to know where you start in order to set a goal.
- You have to know where you came from.
- You have to know who you believe in.
- You have to recognize your own self-worth and self-importance.
- You have to have goals and understand the place your achievements have in your life.
- You have to understand what your definition of success is.
- You have to have self-esteem.
- You have to listen to the wisdom of others.
- You have to understand that you'll never get everything right all of the time, but you will get something right every time.

I've explained some of my past. I came from a rough-and-tumble childhood, if there ever was one—most of which, I have actually left out of this book—so I knew I never wanted anything remotely similar for my own children in terms of lifestyle or circumstances. Financially I never wanted to struggle, so I pushed myself in jobs to close the deal, earn the bonus, and advance to higher ground. It was important to me. I retired at age forty, had time to focus on wellness and exercise, drive the boys to sports practice, have a date night with Danny, and much more. Once I achieved the goals I wanted, that part of my life seemed in balance. But then there was a curve ball.

fly away, butterfly

I was diagnosed with thyroid cancer in October 2012. The prognosis came after a visit to my general practitioner for a regular annual physical. My physician is one of a unique group in his profession—he actually takes time to examine his patients from head to toe. As is his standard practice for patients in their forties, he conducted a sonogram on the arteries in my neck.

As my doctor moved the sonogram transducer around on my neck, he watched the monitor. He'd move slow and then quickly, press harder, slide the device back and forth, and then he stopped. He told me he saw a lump in the area behind my thyroid, a butterfly-shaped gland located near the bottom of the neck that's charged with regulating metabolism, development, and growth. He pointed to the monitor to show me what he was talking about, but of course, all I saw was a blur.

My doctor recommended I go to an imaging center for more tests. I did. The next step was to see an endocrinologist, a doctor who specializes in the study of the endocrine glands such as the thyroid. I met with the endocrinologist a week later, and he assured me the lump that showed up on the sonogram was most likely just a knot. He said not to worry. So I wasn't going to. He shook my hand, and as I was just about to leave the room, he turned to me. He said he changed his mind and suggested we do one more sonogram just for his files. Just to be sure.

He covered the side of my neck with the same jelly grossness that is slopped across the belly of a pregnant woman and ran the transducer back and forth across my skin. But what he saw was something to worry about. His exam revealed that the knot had grown by a full two centimeters in just one week. That was not normal. I'd need a biopsy to determine what was going on. Within moments, he conducted the painful sticking, and I was sent on my way. I felt as if someone had punched me in the neck.

The next day my doctor called with the results—thyroid cancer. It was a hard time. How did I get it? No one else in my family had any problems with their thyroid, at least not that I was aware of. On January 17, 2013, I had surgery to remove my thyroid. The surgery was quick, and everything took place in the morning. While the procedure revealed there was more cancer—six additional nodules—the surgeon was able to remove every last one. My case is considered a victory. I went home that day and posted this to Facebook:

> *At home in bed. Was greeted with bouquets of flowers, boxes of chocolates, enough food to last us a week, magazines, books, tons of cards, text messages, e-mails, sweet FB messages . . . two happy boys, a superman for a husband, and two dancing beagles. Now that the thyroid is*

gone, so is the C-word. (Will get confirmation next week.) Might actually be the best day ever.

On January 28, I received an update on my health. I posted again:

Dancing like James Brown through the halls (at Presbyterian Hospital) with a few tears streaming down my face. Pathology report in: All the bad stuff flew away with the sick butterfly. Cancer free!

What was once out of balance now seemed on an even keel. That's how things roll for all of us, isn't it?

the yin to the yang

Carson and I have what we call an invisible string. It's this unspoken connection that we both feel. We are always together, even when we're apart. But even with an invisible string, as a parent, I have to be sure to let my kids work things out from time to time. I don't believe in enablement. Perhaps it's because I witnessed the way the people in my mother's life enabled her. Even today, my mother relies on financial assistance when she could, truly, make her own way. To be dependent rather than reliant is her choice. But it was perpetuated by members of the family.

Maybe it's overcompensation, or maybe it's hyperawareness, but I never wanted to enable my own children, which is the reason I stay out of things that make sense for me to stay out of, such as not doing Carson's homework so he can be assured an A or not putting away Jack's folded laundry when I could easily do it quicker and neater. I want my kids to stand on their own—to find their own balance.

If you stop and think about your daily life, I'll bet you'll see how often you strive for balance. In marriage, for example, we often marry who we are not. In my marriage, Danny is the introvert, the quiet and more thoughtful one. I'm outspoken and forthright about what I think—a definite extrovert. But we complement each other. He brings me down a notch, and I like to think I push him up one. Recently I had a couple of girlfriends over for dinner, and one asked me if I entertained at my home often. I told her I'd love to—and would do so in a heartbeat—but it was hard to convince Danny because he's perfectly content being at home with me and the boys each and every night.

Balance is more than finding a yin to the yang. It's also recognizing that life is a continuum. It's about giving back in thanks for all that you have. I'm a big believer in the power of the universe—that idea that what goes around comes around. I've been given a lot financially, so I give back financially. I've been given the gift of time, so I volunteer. I serve on boards, consult when I can, and live every day with the mind-set of paying it forward. I'm forever chasing balance. I'll have great parenting days but mess up on other occasions. I'll yell too loudly, ground too severely, or take away the electronics too many times. Then there will be times when I won't correct, won't remind, won't punish. I'll spoil too much, hug too tight, and bake too many chocolate chip cookies. But in the end, I hope it all balances out. Whether it's a marriage, a friendship, a parent, a religion, a sport, a hobby, or a career, I believe you have to identify your foundation—your grounding—so you can work toward balance.

Mother Theresa is so deservedly praised for her kind soul and good deeds. But it's this quote that really gets into my heart: "We should never know all the good that a simple smile can do." I think of this daily. And while my memaw and Mother Teresa couldn't be more opposite in lifestyle and manner, they have said this same thing, each in her own way. It's one of the most pragmatic and simple pieces of advice one could ever get. It's my hope that, as you finish reading this book, you'll find yourself smiling too. Not because I've written something you find funny but rather because you feel a connection to an anecdote or agree with an observation or see an action that resonates—and that realization makes you happy. As for me, I'm happy every day that I've had the ability to write this book. And by that I mean that I'm happy to have had all of these experiences, careers, friends, and family that have all swirled together to help me tell this story. It's a large part of my own balancing act. My personal course has helped me to observe and make sense of the crazy goodness in every moment of parenthood.

Life is ironic. It is a puzzling joy to look back at struggles and to understand why they even happened in the first place. Some of the things that happened didn't make sense to me then—and still don't today. But other things have made profound sense and have provided me with choices, character insight, and a clear light on how to live my life, and how I should influence my children to live theirs.

It's important to see the opportunity presented by a school grade of "D," the obliteration of a brand-new TV screen, and even a terrifying health scare. It's the bumps that make us who we are. The easy stuff is cake. We wouldn't know how to glide without falling face first. It all confirms to me that when building character, it's best to just roll with it.

about the author

Kim Garrett retired from Facebook at forty after four years as Director of National Sales, central region. In this career-changing role, Kim helped Facebook define its social strategies, build brand presence, and evolve into one of the most popular and influential social media companies in the world. Kim's professional experience includes working for the Dallas Cowboys, House of Blues, and Clear Channel. Today Kim provides consulting and advisory management to early-stage companies and causes near to her heart. She's a sports enthusiast, yoga student, foodie, and banjo player. She loves travel, adventure, and the wonder of motherhood.

Kim lives in Dallas with her husband Danny and their boys, Carson and Jack.